SKYBOX PRESS

LaCroix

CCM

VISIT
LAUDERDALE
88

HYP2RLITE
VAPOR
TRUE
19
PANTHERS
BAUER
FIT.
CELSIUS
FORSLING
42

PANTHERS
12
17
CCM
BAUER

TRUE
PANTHERS
33
41

MPIONS
PANTHERS

REGULAR SEASON	FIRST ROUND VS. TAMPA BAY LIGHTNING	SECOND ROUND VS. TORONTO MAPLE LEAFS
16	38	52

EASTERN CONFERENCE FINAL

VS.

CAROLINA HURRICANES

70

STANLEY CUP FINAL

VS.

EDMONTON OILERS

88

TKACHUK

PANTHERS

LAS O
FLORIDA
FLORIDA PANTHERS
championship
CELEBRATION
PRESENTED BY VISIT LAUDERDALE
BIGBUS.COM
Bus
9
GO CATS GO
SHERIFF
SHERIFF
NORTH
A1A

LVD
CCM
POLICE

REGULAR SEASON

FINAL 2024-25 REGULAR SEASON STANDINGS

EASTERN CONFERENCE

ATLANTIC DIVISION	W	L	OT	PTS
TORONTO MAPLE LEAFS	52	26	4	108
TAMPA BAY LIGHTNING	47	27	8	102
FLORIDA PANTHERS	47	31	4	98
OTTAWA SENATORS	45	30	7	97
MONTRÉAL CANADIENS	40	31	11	91
DETROIT RED WINGS	39	35	8	86
BUFFALO SABRES	36	39	7	79
BOSTON BRUINS	33	39	10	76

METROPOLITAN DIVISION	W	L	OT	PTS
WASHINGTON CAPITALS	51	22	9	111
CAROLINA HURRICANES	47	30	5	99
NEW JERSEY DEVILS	42	33	7	91
COLUMBUS BLUE JACKETS	40	33	9	89
NEW YORK RANGERS	39	36	7	85
NEW YORK ISLANDERS	35	35	12	82
PITTSBURGH PENGUINS	34	36	12	80
PHILADELPHIA FLYERS	33	39	10	76

WESTERN CONFERENCE

CENTRAL DIVISION	W	L	OT	PTS
WINNIPEG JETS	56	22	4	116
DALLAS STARS	50	26	6	106
COLORADO AVALANCHE	49	29	4	102
MINNESOTA WILD	45	30	7	97
ST. LOUIS BLUES	44	30	8	96
UTAH HOCKEY CLUB	38	31	13	89
NASHVILLE PREDATORS	30	44	8	68
CHICAGO BLACKHAWKS	25	46	11	61

PACIFIC DIVISION	W	L	OT	PTS
VEGAS GOLDEN KNIGHTS	50	22	10	110
LOS ANGELES KINGS	48	25	9	105
EDMONTON OILERS	48	29	5	101
CALGARY FLAMES	41	27	14	96
VANCOUVER CANUCKS	38	30	14	90
ANAHEIM DUCKS	35	37	10	80
SEATTLE KRAKEN	35	41	6	76
SAN JOSE SHARKS	20	50	12	52

The Panthers celebrate their first win under their new Stanley Cup Champions banner at Amerant Bank Arena following their 6–4 season-opening win over the Boston Bruins on October 7, 2024.

AMERANT BANK ARENA
CATS WIN YOU WIN
CATS WIN
YOU WIN
BUY ONE 3-TENDER MEAL
GET ONE FREE!
00.0
3RD PERIOD
SHOTS ON GOAL
28 35
4
6
$50,195
$50,195
HUIZENGA
37
TORREY
93
2024
AutoNation
HONDA
COMCAST BUSINESS
AMAZING
CATS WIN YOU WIN
THE AMERANT VAULT
AMERANT
SEMINOLE CASINO
VERHAEGHE
23
MARCHAND
63
TKACHUK
REINHART
13
KAMMER

Gustav Forsling shows his family his Stanley Cup championship ring at the Panthers' ring ceremony at War Memorial Auditorium on October 7, 2024.

Anton Lundell, Aleksander Barkov, Niko Mikkola, and Eetu Luostarinen get a photo with their new Stanley Cup championship rings alongside the trophy itself.

EASTERN CONFERENCE CHAMPIONS 2022-23
ATLANTIC DIVISION CHAMPIONS 2023-24
EASTERN CONFERENCE CHAMPIONS 2023-24
LUONGO 1
HUIZENGA 37
TORREY 93
STANLEY CUP CHAMPIONS
FLORIDA
2024
AutoNation
CELSIUS
STANLEY CUP CHAMPIONS

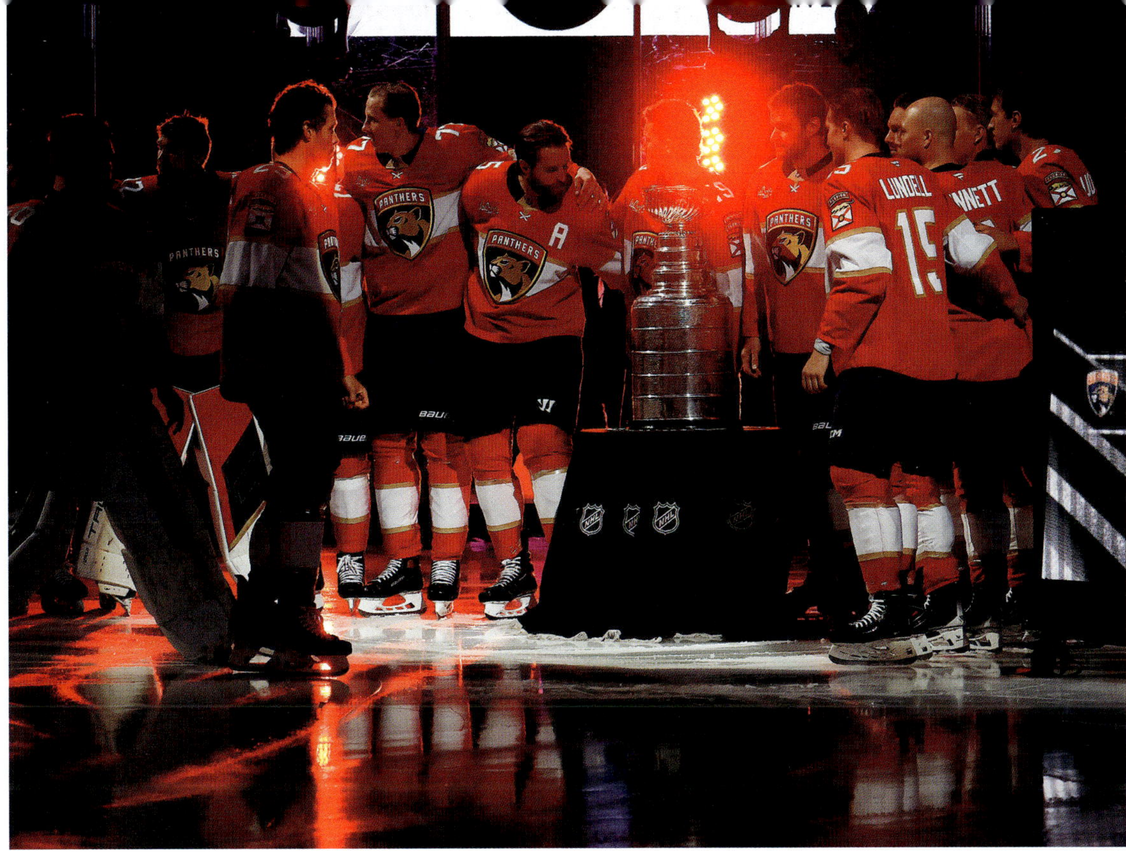

OPPOSITE
The Panthers' Stanley Cup champions banner is raised during a pregame ceremony at Amerant Bank Arena on October 8, 2024.

TOP
The Panthers huddle around the Stanley Cup prior to the championship banner raising.

BOTTOM
Sam Reinhart completes an acrobatic flip after scoring a highlight reel goal in Florida's season-opening win over the Bruins.

ABOVE
Aleksander Barkov and Sam Reinhart celebrate Reinhart's season-opening goal against the Bruins.

ABOVE
The Panthers and the Columbus Blue Jackets honored Johnny and Matthew Gaudreau in a pregame banner raising ceremony at Nationwide Arena on October 15, 2024.

OPPOSITE
Sam Bennett and the entire Panthers and Blue Jackets teams wore #13 Gaudreau jerseys during warmups prior to the game.

GAUDREAU
13
ZZA

GET PULLED
SOBER OR
PULLED OVER
35
THEODORE
FORSLING
42

OPPOSITE
Gustav Forsling scores the overtime winner over the Vegas Golden Knights on October 19.

BELOW
On October 25, the Panthers and Vincent J. Viola, Chairman, Owner, and Governor of the Florida Panthers brought the Stanley Cup to Viola's alma mater, the US Military Academy at West Point.

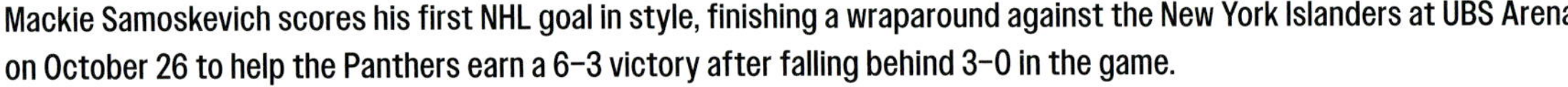

Mackie Samoskevich scores his first NHL goal in style, finishing a wraparound against the New York Islanders at UBS Arena on October 26 to help the Panthers earn a 6–3 victory after falling behind 3–0 in the game.

TOP
The Panthers enter Nokia Arena in Tampere, Finland, wearing custom sauna robes in a tribute to Finnish culture.

BOTTOM
A net camera angle of the first of two goals (and four points) by Aleksander Barkov scored in his hometown of Tampere, which helped the Panthers to a series sweep in the 2024 NHL Global Series.

ABOVE
Matthew Tkachuk celebrates after scoring against the Dallas Stars in the 2024 NHL Global Series.

16
FLORIDA
C
BAUER
35
TRUE

OPPOSITE

Aleksander Barkov finishes a between-the-legs deke in the shootout to help the Cats to a victory over the Seattle Kraken on December 10 at Climate Pledge Arena.

BELOW

Sam Bennett celebrates with Sam Reinhart after Reinhart scored a goal off the mask of Edmonton Oilers goaltender Stuart Skinner in a thrilling 6–5 win at Rogers Place on December 16.

Nate Schmidt works to clear the net in front of Sergei Bobrovsky in a game against the Carolina Hurricanes.

Aaron Ekblad carries the puck against the San Jose Sharks in a 7–2 Panthers victory at SAP Center.

A.J. Greer lays a hit on Vegas Golden Knights defenseman Brayden McNabb.

In a pregame ceremony on February 2, the Panthers celebrated Dmitry Kulikov reaching his 1,000th NHL game.

TRUMP
47

OPPOSITE
Aleksander Barkov and Matthew Tkachuk present US President Donald J. Trump with a custom jersey and a gold-plated stick during the Panthers' ceremonial visit to the White House on February 3.

TOP
Matthew Tkachuk celebrates after scoring a game-winning goal against his hometown St. Louis Blues with 12 seconds remaining on February 6.

BOTTOM
Seth Jones gets low to block a shot in his Panthers debut against the Tampa Bay Lightning on March 3.

ABOVE
Nico Sturm deflects the puck on net in his Panthers debut against the Buffalo Sabres on March 8.

ABOVE
Vitek Vanecek stopped all 21 shots he faced in his Panthers debut against the Buffalo Sabres on March 8.

TOP
Brad Marchand battles for the puck in his Panthers debut against Utah on March 28. Marchand would earn the primary assist on Sam Bennett's OT winner in the game.

BOTTOM
Marchand scores his first goal as a Panther against the Detroit Red Wings on April 10.

Plantation, FL native Jaycob Megna battles Buffalo Sabres forward Peyton Krebs on April 12.

FIRST ROUND

vs.

TAMPA BAY

LIGHTNING

GAME 1

6-2

FLA leads 1-0

GAME 2

2-0

FLA leads 2-0

GAME 3

5-1

FLA leads 2-1

GAME 4

4-2

FLA leads 3-1

GAME 5

6-3

FLA wins 4-1

SERIES STATS

NO.	PLAYER	GP	G	A	PTS	+/-
13	SAM REINHART	5	2	4	6	+2
9	SAM BENNETT	5	3	2	5	+1
15	ANTON LUNDELL	5	2	3	5	+3
16	ALEKSANDER BARKOV	5	1	4	5	+2
19	MATTHEW TKACHUK	5	3	2	5	+1
27	EETU LUOSTARINEN	5	1	4	5	+6
63	BRAD MARCHAND	5	0	4	4	+5
23	CARTER VERHAEGHE	5	2	1	3	+1
88	NATE SCHMIDT	5	3	0	3	+4
3	SETH JONES	5	1	1	2	+5
7	DMITRY KULIKOV	5	0	2	2	0
5	AARON EKBLAD	2	1	0	1	-3

NO.	PLAYER	GP	G	A	PTS	+/-
17	EVAN RODRIGUES	5	0	1	1	0
25	MACKIE SAMOSKEVICH	3	0	1	1	0
42	GUSTAV FORSLING	5	0	1	1	+1
8	NICO STURM	5	0	0	0	-2
10	A.J. GREER	2	0	0	0	-3
70	JESPER BOQVIST	5	0	0	0	-2
26	UVIS BALINSKIS	3	0	0	0	+3
77	NIKO MIKKOLA	5	0	0	0	+1
92	TOMAS NOSEK	0	0	0	0	0
12	JONAH GADJOVICH	0	0	0	0	0
6	JAYCOB MEGNA	0	0	0	0	0

NO.	GOALIE	GP	W/L	GA	SA	SV	SV%	GAA	SO
72	SERGEI BOBROVSKY	5	4/1	11	111	100	.901	2.21	1
41	VITEK VANECEK	0	0/0	0	0	0	0	0	0

CCM
88
BAUER

TKACHUK
19
88
81
13
BAUER
CCM
VAPOR

OPPOSITE
Matthew Tkachuk scores on Andrei Vasilevskiy in Game 1 of the First Round of the 2025 Stanley Cup Playoffs against the Tampa Bay Lightning.

BELOW
Sergei Bobrovsky stopped all 19 Lightning shots he faced in Game 2 to earn the shutout and propel the Cats to a 2–0 series lead.

Game 3
PRESENTED BY
PLAYOFFS 2025 • ROUND 1 • GAME 3
07:52
PRE-GAME
0
$37,530
Round 1
Game 3
DISNEY DESCENDANTS SEP 6
AMERANT
DISCOVER
ESPN BET
Energizer
FANDUEL
CAT
CAT
Great Clips
Enterprise
AutoNation
PEPSI
HONDA

ANK
AMERANT
$37,530
37
93
AMERANT
BODYARMOR
FASTENAL
SAP
SAP
Expedia
GEICO
NAVY FEDERAL
BETMGM

TOP
Matthew Tkachuk scores a goal in Game 3.

BOTTOM
Anton Lundell celebrates with Nate Schmidt and Dmitry Kulikov after scoring the opening goal in Game 4.

OPPOSITE
Aaron Ekblad scores the game-tying goal in Game 4 with 3:47 remaining in regulation. Seth Jones would tally 11 seconds later to propel the Panthers to a 3–1 series lead.

88
Advent Health
BAUER
bauer
5

23
PANTHERS
77
C
Advent Health
BRANDT
21
88
MOSER
90
BAUER
CCM

OPPOSITE
Carter Verhaeghe battles for position in front of the Lightning net. Verhaeghe tallied the empty-net goal in Game 4.

BELOW
Sergei Bobrovsky stretches for a highlight reel save against Lightning forward Gage Goncalves in Game 5.

ABOVE

Aleksander Barkov deflects a Gustav Forsling shot past Andrei Vasilevskiy in Game 5 to give the Panthers a 3–2 lead in the game.

OPPOSITE

Anton Lundell deflects a Brad Marchand pass into the Lightning net in Game 5.

88
LUNDELL
15
bauer
CCM
27
CIRELLI
71

SECOND ROUND

VS.
TORONTO
MAPLE LEAFS

GAME 1	GAME 2
5-4	4-3
TOR leads 1-0	TOR leads 2-0

GAME 3 OT	GAME 4
5-4	2-0
TOR leads 2-1	Series tied 2-2

GAME 5	GAME 6
6-1	2-0
FLA leads 3-2	Series tied 3-3

GAME 7
6-1
FLA wins 4-3

SERIES STATS

NO.	PLAYER	GP	G	A	PTS	+/-
63	BRAD MARCHAND	7	3	5	8	+6
27	EETU LUOSTARINEN	7	2	5	7	+5
13	SAM REINHART	7	2	3	5	+1
15	ANTON LUNDELL	7	2	3	5	+6
16	ALEKSANDER BARKOV	7	2	3	5	+2
23	CARTER VERHAEGHE	7	2	3	5	0
5	AARON EKBLAD	6	1	4	5	+6
9	SAM BENNETT	7	3	1	4	-2
19	MATTHEW TKACHUK	7	0	4	4	0
3	SETH JONES	7	2	2	4	+1
88	NATE SCHMIDT	7	0	4	4	0
12	JONAH GADJOVICH	5	2	1	3	+3
17	EVAN RODRIGUES	5	0	3	3	-1
10	A.J. GREER	6	1	1	2	+2
70	JESPER BOQVIST	4	1	1	2	-1
7	DMITRY KULIKOV	7	1	1	2	-1
26	UVIS BALINSKIS	1	1	0	1	+1
42	GUSTAV FORSLING	7	0	1	1	+5
77	NIKO MIKKOLA	7	1	0	1	+1
92	TOMAS NOSEK	5	0	1	1	+3
8	NICO STURM	2	0	0	0	-1
25	MACKIE SAMOSKEVICH	1	0	0	0	0
6	JAYCOB MEGNA	0	0	0	0	0

NO.	GOALIE	GP	W/L	GA	SA	SV	SV%	GAA	SO
72	SERGEI BOBROVSKY	7	4/3	17	173	156	.902	2.39	1
41	VITEK VANECEK	0	0/0	0	0	0	0	0	0

83
BARKOV
16
MATTHEWS
34
CCM

FLORIDA
17
BAUER
TORONTO
CCM
otic

OPPOSITE
Evan Rodrigues carries the puck up the ice past Maple Leafs forward John Tavares in Game 1 of the Second Round of the 2025 Stanley Cup Playoffs.

TOP
Sam Reinhart battles for the puck with Maple Leafs blueliner Oliver Ekman-Larsson.

BOTTOM
Aaron Ekblad and Gustav Forsling position themselves to block a shot against the Maple Leafs.

ABOVE
Anton Lundell celebrates with Aaron Ekblad after scoring in Game 2 to tie the score at three goals each.

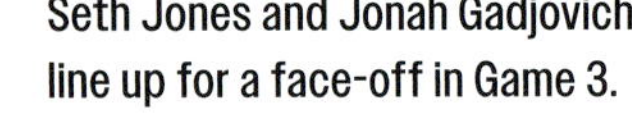

Seth Jones and Jonah Gadjovich line up for a face-off in Game 3.

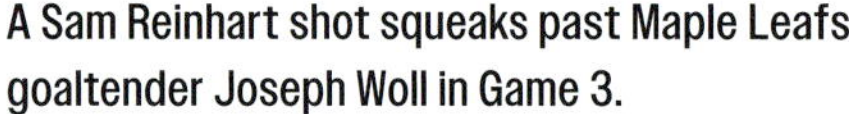

A Sam Reinhart shot squeaks past Maple Leafs goaltender Joseph Woll in Game 3.

Aleksander Barkov scores Florida's first goal in Game 3 against the Maple Leafs, sparking a multigoal comeback that would bring the Panthers back into the series.

ABOVE
Carter Verhaeghe buries a backhand feed from Sam Bennett to tie Game 3 at three goals each.

OPPOSITE
Brad Marchand moves up the ice against Maple Leafs forward Steven Lorentz.

18
WARRIOR
63
PANTHERS

BENNETT
9
60
BAUER
BAUER
BAUER
BAUER
BAUER
WARRIOR
WARRIOR
TORONTO MAPLE LEAFS

OPPOSITE
Sam Bennett scores on Joseph Woll in Game 4 to put the Cats up 2–0, which ended as the game's final score.

BELOW
Sergei Bobrovsky stopped all 23 Maple Leafs shots in Game 4 to earn his second of three shutouts in the 2025 postseason.

ABOVE
Sam Reinhart fires the puck on net against the Maple Leafs.

TOP
Niko Mikkola celebrates after scoring a goal in Game 5.

BOTTOM
Dmitry Kulikov celebrates with his teammates after scoring in Game 5.

Jesper Boqvist celebrates after scoring his first goal of the playoffs in Game 5.

ABOVE
Niko Mikkola celebrates with Seth Jones after scoring a goal in Game 5.

OPPOSITE
Sergei Bobrovsky makes a sliding stop on Maple Leafs forward Scott Laughton in Game 7.

27
BAUER
TRUE
72
PANTHERS
24

FLORIDA
RIELLY
44
25
60
BAUER
CCM

OPPOSITE

Jonah Gadjovich celebrates after scoring a goal in Game 7 to put the Cats up 3–0.

BELOW

The Panthers and the Maple Leafs shake hands following a hard-fought second-round series. Florida would move on to face a familiar foe in the conference final.

EASTERN CONFERENCE FINAL

vs.
CAROLINA
HURRICANES

GAME 1
5-2
FLA leads 1-0

GAME 2
5-0
FLA leads 2-0

GAME 3
6-2
FLA leads 3-0

GAME 4
3-0
FLA leads 3-1

GAME 5
5-3
FLA wins 4-1

SERIES STATS

NO.	PLAYER	GP	G	A	PTS	+/-
9	SAM BENNETT	5	4	3	7	+3
16	ALEKSANDER BARKOV	5	3	4	7	0
17	EVAN RODRIGUES	5	1	6	7	+3
19	MATTHEW TKACHUK	5	2	5	7	+3
23	CARTER VERHAEGHE	5	2	4	6	+3
5	AARON EKBLAD	5	1	4	5	+3
77	NIKO MIKKOLA	4	2	2	4	+5
70	JESPER BOQVIST	2	1	2	3	+3
13	SAM REINHART	3	0	2	2	+1
15	ANTON LUNDELL	5	1	1	2	+3
63	BRAD MARCHAND	5	1	1	2	0
42	GUSTAV FORSLING	5	1	1	2	+4
92	TOMAS NOSEK	5	0	2	2	+2
10	A.J. GREER	4	1	0	1	+1
27	EETU LUOSTARINEN	5	1	0	1	0
3	SETH JONES	5	0	1	1	+3
8	NICO STURM	1	0	0	0	0
12	JONAH GADJOVICH	5	0	0	0	+2
7	DMITRY KULIKOV	5	0	0	0	+2
26	UVIS BALINSKIS	1	0	0	0	0
88	NATE SCHMIDT	5	0	0	0	0
25	MACKIE SAMOSKEVICH	0	0	0	0	0
6	JAYCOB MEGNA	0	0	0	0	0

NO.	GOALIE	GP	W/L	GA	SA	SV	SV%	GAA	SO
72	SERGEI BOBROVSKY	5	4/1	8	124	116	.935	1.60	1
41	VITEK VANECEK	0	0/0	0	0	0	0	0	0

16
3
CCM
BARKOV
AutoNation
C
FLORIDA
FLORIDA
PANTHERS
CCM

Gustav Forsling moves to block a shot from Carolina Hurricanes defenseman Shayne Gostisbehere in Game 1 of the Eastern Conference Final.

Brad Marchand and Evan Rodrigues look on as Sam Bennett's shot enters the Carolina net in Game 1, putting the Cats up 4–1 in the game.

ABOVE
A.J. Greer throws his hands in the air after lighting the lamp in Game 1 on a cross-crease feed from Niko Mikkola.

TOP
Sergei Bobrovsky makes a split save against the Hurricanes in Game 2. He stopped all 17 shots he faced in the game for his third shutout of the postseason.

BOTTOM
Matthew Tkachuk and Hurricanes forward Sebastian Aho are separated by a linesman.

Sam Bennett scores his second goal of the game in Game 2, off a feed from Carter Verhaeghe.

FLORIDA
CCM
FASTENAL

OPPOSITE
Seth Jones hits Hurricanes captain Jordan Staal into the boards.

TOP
Niko Mikkola deflects the puck in off Hurricanes defenseman Dmitry Orlov for Florida's first goal in Game 3.

ABOVE
Sergei Bobrovsky stretches for a save on Hurricanes forward Logan Stankoven in Game 3.

BOTTOM
Mikkola wires the puck past Frederik Andersen for his second goal of the game in Game 3.

BALINSKIS
26
VERHAEGHE
23
BENNETT
9

MARCHAND
63
BARKOV
16
TKACHUK
19

Dmitry Kulikov hits Jordan Staal into the boards.

A net camera angle of Niko Mikkola's first goal of the game in Game 3.

Seth Jones fires a shot on net in Game 3.

Lenovo
ROBINSON
50
cketmas
21
TRUE
ERSEN

OPPOSITE
Carter Verhaeghe shoots the puck past Frederik Andersen after an elite pass from Aleksander Barkov, putting Florida up 4–3 in Game 5 with 7:39 remaining.

BELOW
Sam Bennett celebrates with his teammates after burying an empty-net goal in Game 5, ensuring Florida's third consecutive trip to the Stanley Cup Final.

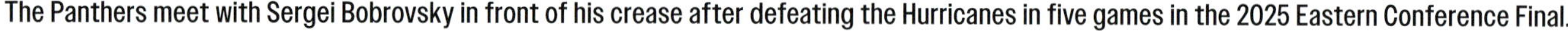

The Panthers meet with Sergei Bobrovsky in front of his crease after defeating the Hurricanes in five games in the 2025 Eastern Conference Final.

The Panthers players and staff surround the Prince of Wales Trophy for a celebratory photo for the third consecutive year.

STANLEY CUP FINAL

vs.
EDMONTON
OILERS

GAME 1 OT	GAME 2 2OT
4-3	5-4
EDM leads 1-0	Series tied 1-1

GAME 3	GAME 4 OT
6-1	5-4
FLA leads 2-1	Series tied 2-2

GAME 5	GAME 6
5-2	5-1
FLA leads 3-2	FLA wins 4-2

SERIES STATS

NO.	PLAYER	GP	G	A	PTS	+/-
13	SAM REINHART	6	7	3	10	+1
23	CARTER VERHAEGHE	6	1	8	9	+8
19	MATTHEW TKACHUK	6	3	4	7	+3
9	SAM BENNETT	6	5	1	6	+4
15	ANTON LUNDELL	6	1	5	6	+7
27	EETU LUOSTARINEN	6	1	5	6	0
63	BRAD MARCHAND	6	6	0	6	+6
16	ALEKSANDER BARKOV	6	0	5	5	0
88	NATE SCHMIDT	6	0	5	5	+3
17	EVAN RODRIGUES	6	1	3	4	+1
3	SETH JONES	6	1	1	2	+2
5	AARON EKBLAD	6	1	1	2	+4

NO.	PLAYER	GP	G	A	PTS	+/-
7	DMITRY KULIKOV	6	1	0	1	+5
42	GUSTAV FORSLING	6	0	1	1	+3
77	NIKO MIKKOLA	6	0	1	1	-2
70	JESPER BOQVIST	2	0	0	0	+1
12	JONAH GADJOVICH	6	0	0	0	-2
10	A.J. GREER	4	0	0	0	-2
92	TOMAS NOSEK	6	0	0	0	-1
25	MACKIE SAMOSKEVICH	0	0	0	0	0
8	NICO STURM	0	0	0	0	0
6	JAYCOB MEGNA	0	0	0	0	0
26	UVIS BALINSKIS	0	0	0	0	0

NO.	GOALIE	GP	W/L	GA	SA	SV	SV%	GAA	SO
72	SERGEI BOBROVSKY	6	4/2	17	210	193	.919	2.45	0
41	VITEK VANECEK	0	0/0	0	0	0	0	0	0

CAT
CAT
BODYARMOR
SPORTS DRINK
SAFEWAY
PERRY
90

88
CCM
FLORIDA
AutoNation
WARRIOR
FLORIDA
23
BAUER

OPPOSITE
Brad Marchand celebrates with Nate Schmidt and Carter Verhaeghe after scoring a power-play goal in Game 1 of the 2025 Stanley Cup Final against the Edmonton Oilers.

BELOW
Sam Bennett snipes the puck past Oilers goaltender Stuart Skinner for his second goal of the game in Game 1.

ABOVE
Sergei Bobrovsky denies Trent Frederic on the doorstep in overtime of Game 1.

OPPOSITE
Evan Rodrigues battles for position with Oilers captain Connor McDavid.

CCM
97
17
BAUER
PANTHERS

Brad Marchand leaps into the air after scoring the game-winning goal in double overtime of Game 2 while Anton Lundell and Jesper Boqvist start to celebrate.

Panthers Head Coach Paul Maurice and Assistant Coach Jamie Kompon on the Florida bench in Game 2.

BOBROVSKY
97
TRUE
BAUER
CCM
CCM

OPPOSITE
Sergei Bobrovsky denies Connor McDavid in the crease.

BELOW
Matthew Tkachuk and Darnell Nurse battle by the glass.

ABOVE
Seth Jones buries a goal in Game 2 after a smooth cross-ice pass from Eetu Luostarinen.

OPPOSITE
The Panthers faithful carry the flag prior to the start of Game 3 of the Stanley Cup Final at Amerant Bank Arena.

TORREY
93
THE AMERANT VAULT
AMERANT
upper level
Great Clips
enterprise
MassMutual
BODYARMOR
SPORTS DRINK
SAP
SAP
Expedia
GEICO
NAVY FEDERAL

Carter Verhaeghe celebrates after scoring a goal over the shoulder of Stuart Skinner in Game 3, putting the Cats up 2–0.

Sam Bennett's teammates surround him after he buries his 14th goal of the playoffs in Game 3, capping off a shift that saw him dish out two big hits before being sprung by Eetu Luostarinen for a breakaway.

Eetu Luostarinen battles for position against Connor Brown.

Matthew Tkachuk greets Sergei Bobrovsky after Florida's 6–1 win in Game 3.

BOBBY
BOBBY
NOSEK
92
PANTHERS
PANTHERS
DRAFT
SPORTS
Expedi
BAUER
CCM

CASINO
LUNDELL
15
PANTHERS
CCM
BAUER

Sergei Bobrovsky stretches for a save in Game 5.

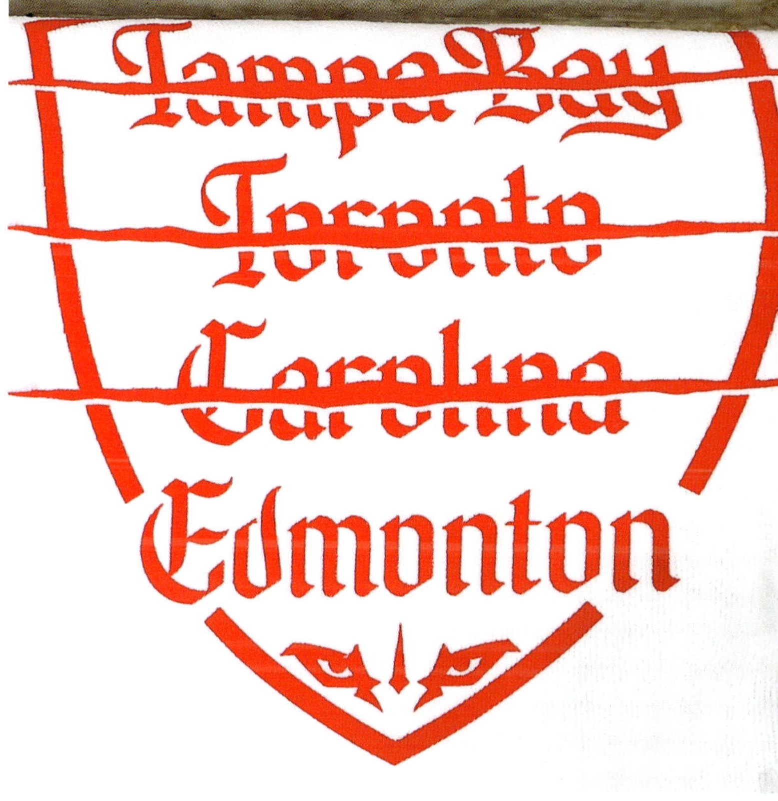

TOP
Brad Marchand squeezes the puck past Calvin Pickard while Oilers defenseman Jake Walman falls into the crease. Marchand's goal was his second of the game, giving the Cats a 3–0 lead.

BOTTOM
Eetu Luostarinen celebrates after scoring the empty-net goal to secure Florida's 5–2 victory in Game 5, sending the Panthers back to South Florida with a chance to win the Stanley Cup on home ice for the second consecutive season.

ABOVE
A Florida Panthers rally towel displaying the teams Florida played in the 2025 Stanley Cup Playoffs.

SKINNER
PANTHERS

OPPOSITE
Sam Reinhart slides on the ice after firing the puck past Stuart Skinner, completing a highlight-reel goal to open Game 6.

BELOW
Reinhart deflects the puck past Skinner for his second of four goals in Game 6, becoming the second player in NHL history with four tallies in a Cup-clinching win, propelling the Panthers past the Oilers in a dominant 5–1 win to once again lift the Stanley Cup at Amerant Bank Arena.

ABOVE
The Panthers throw their equipment into the air and begin to rush Sergei Bobrovsky as the clock hits zero in Game 6.

OPPOSITE
Celebratory streamers rain down throughout Amerant Bank Arena as the Panthers celebrate on the ice and Cats fans rejoice in the stands.

STANLEY CUP CHAMPIONS
SEMINOLE CASINO
Expedia
AstraZeneca
GEICO
MGM
DEX imaging

MPIONS

OPPOSITE
Sam Bennett lifts the Conn Smythe Trophy, presented annually to the most valuable player for his team in the playoffs. Bennett led the playoffs with 15 goals, including an NHL-record 13 tallies on the road.

BELOW
NHL Commissioner Gary Bettman hands the Stanley Cup off to Aleksander Barkov at Amerant Bank Arena for the second year in a row.

STANLEY CUP
Champions
2025
ANTHERS
FLORIDA
NHL
NTHERS
STANLEY CUP
Champions
2025

STANLEY CUP
Champions
2025
FLORIDA
NHL
LaCroix
STANLEY CUP
Champions
2025
FLORIDA
STANLEY CUP
Champions
2025
FLORIDA
STANLEY CUP
Champions
2025
FLORIDA

ABOVE

Nate Schmidt lifts the Stanley Cup in the Panthers locker room after Game 6. Schmidt produced 12 points (3-9-12) in 23 postseason games with Florida.

OPPOSITE

Carter Verhaeghe lifts the Stanley Cup after becoming a three-time Stanley Cup champion.

FLORIDA
20
25
FLORIDA PANTHERS

FLORIDA
FLORIDA PANTHERS
championship
CELEBRATION
PRESENTED BY VISIT LAUDERDALE
POLICE
POLICE
POLICE
SHERIFF
SHERIFF

Air Pros
OFFICIAL AC COMPANY OF THE FLORIDA PANTHERS
POLICE

Panthers Head Athletic Trainer Dave DiNapoli lifts the Stanley Cup at the Panthers Championship Celebration.

South Florida bagpipe bands led the way at the Panthers Championship Celebration.

Anton Lundell, Panthers Vice President of Player Engagement Mike Huff, and Niko Mikkola on top of one of the buses.

Sam Reinhart parties with the South Florida faithful.

PANTHERS
REIGNING
CHAMPS
2024
FLORIDA
2025

OPPOSITE
Brad Marchand lifts the Stanley Cup in front of Panthers fans lining the streets of A1A.

TOP
Sam Bennett lifts the Stanley Cup after giving his speech to the crowd.

BOTTOM
Matthew Tkachuk and Sam Reinhart on one of the buses at the Panthers Championship Celebration.

ABOVE
A custom crown fitted with a symbol of the Florida Panthers: a plastic rat.

PANTHERS
GEICO
STANLEY CUP CHAMPIONS
2025
PEPSI
BARKOV
16

PANTHERS
2025

ABOVE

On May 31, 2025, the entire Panthers team took part in the inaugural Gaudreau Family 5K to honor the life and legacy of Johnny Gaudreau and his brother, Matthew.

OPPOSITE

A closer look at the Gaudreau Family 5K shirt that all members of the Panthers wore during the walk, which raised money for an adaptive playground at Archbishop Damiano School, a special-needs school in Westville, New Jersey.

THE GAUDREAU FAMILY
GAUDREAU
1st Annual 5K Run/Walk

FLORIDA PANTHERS

Lauren Cochran
Janine Kurpiel
Brett Maurer
Chrissy Parente
Thomas Harding
Adelyn Biedenbach

SKYBOX PRESS

Editor & Publisher
Scott Gummer

Design
SeeSullivan

Copyeditor
Mark Nichol

Skybox Press wishes to thank Jennifer Kallas with the National Hockey League and Carmin Romanelli, Michael Klein, Mark Awad, and Daniel Romo with Getty Images.

PHOTOGRAPHY

NATIONAL HOCKEY LEAGUE: Brian Babineau, Mark Blinch, Michael Chisholm, Andy Devlin, Josh Lavallee, Mark LoMoglio, Christopher Mast, Andre Ringuette, Scott Rovak, Eliot J. Schechter, Thomas Skrlj, Kevin Sousa, Paul Swanson; **GETTY IMAGES SPORT**: Claus Andersen, Joel Auerbach, Bruce Bennett, Mike Carlson, Steph Chambers, Leila Devlin, Carmen Mandato, Codie McLachlan, Christian Petersen, Eliot J. Schechter, Jared C. Tilton, Jeff Vinnick, Candice Ward; **GETTY IMAGES NEWS**: Kevin Dietsch; **TRIBUNE NEWS SERVICE**: Miami Herald, Sun Sentinel; Icon Sportswire.

Additional photography courtesy of the Lauren Sopourn and the Florida Panthers.

www.skyboxpress.com
info@skyboxpress.com

ISBN: 979-8-9921084-7-7

Printed in the United States of America

10 9 8 7 6 5 4 3 2 1

Published by Skybox Press, LLC.